To my boys

Jade

Remember me this way

HandE Publishers
LONDON

Published by HandE Publishers Ltd
Epping Film Studios, Brickfield Business Centre,
Thornwood High Road, Epping, CM16 6TH
www.handepublishers.co.uk

First published in the United Kingdom 2009
First Edition

ISBN 978-1-906873-26-4

A CIP catalogue record for this book is available from
The British Library

Photography by Simon Bridger and Danny Hayward
Cover design by Ruth Mahoney
Typeset by Ruth Mahoney

Printed and bound in England
by Butler Tanner and Dennis

MARIE CURIE CANCER CARE

MARIE Curie Cancer Care is a leading UK charity providing free nursing care for terminally ill patients who wish to spend their final days at home instead of in hospital. The charity's nurses now look after half of all UK cancer patients who make that choice. They also provide free practical and emotional support for patient's families and/or carers.

The charity is the biggest provider of hospice care outside the NHS with nine hospices around the country.

Every year the charity cares for around 27,000 patients and needs to raise over £115 million.

On behalf of 'MatrixPhotos.com Ltd', HandE Publishers will donate a minimum of £10,000 from the sales of this book to Marie Curie Cancer Care to help provide more nursing care for terminally ill patients.

You can donate at **www.mariecurie.org.uk** or by calling the free-phone donation line 0800 716 146.

Charity registration no. 207994 (England and Wales) and SC038731 (Scotland)

TO Bobby and Freddie,

I have asked for this book to be made so that when you are older you can remember just how much fun we had together.

I thank God that we made the most of all our time together and I treasure the moments we shared. I know that with the help of nanny Jackiey, Jack and daddy Jeff you will turn into fine, upstanding young men.

We had so many wonderful adventures together, from horse-riding and fishing in Wales to camel rides in the desert of Abu Dhabi and water fights at Butlins.

These are my most precious memories, and this book will be your keepsake so that you will always remember those good times.

Some person much wiser than me once said that if you never discover something you would die for, then you haven't lived.

Well, you are both proof that I have lived. I will love you always.

Mummy.

Simon Bridger

Danny Hayward

Foreword

DANNY Hayward and Simon Bridger of MatrixPhotos.com, one of London's biggest celebrity picture agencies, have been taking pictures of Jade since she entered the Big Brother house back in 2002.

We built up a close relationship with the star, which was personal as well as professional.

We followed her through some amazing highs and terrible lows – including, of course, her brave battle with cancer. The unparalleled access she granted us has led to some of the most famous pictures seen in the pages of the National Press.

It was a journey which took in family holidays, panto appearances, launches for perfumes and books and amazing trips such as the visit to India following Celebrity Big Brother that produced such memorable images. We are truly grateful to our wives Victoria and Caroline for putting up with the endless foreign excursions Jade led us on!

We have captured exclusively thousands of tender family moments with Jade's cherished boys Bobby and Freddie as well as with her true love, Jack. There were thousands more wonderfully humorous pictures taken with her many close friends.

None of the many celebrities we have photographed over the years has been as canny as Jade in understanding the value of a brilliant picture. And we have had great fun playing cat-and-mouse with other photographers to keep her away from their lenses!

This book is a tribute to a very special lady and the relationship we shared. We are proud it will raise money for Marie Curie Cancer Care, the charity she chose.

Jade, we will always remember you.

Simon Bridger and Danny Hayward,
MatrixPhotos.com

THE Sun

bizarre
READERS
POLL 2002

Well done to...
Jade Goody

Best Reality TV Star

Foreword

JADE Goody was tabloid gold. A down-to-Earth, working-class girl who pulled no punches, spoke her mind, had boundless energy, good cheer and an insatiable lust for life.

She filled hundreds of pages of The Sun during seven years in the public eye. Our readers couldn't get enough. She was one of us: an ordinary person, thrust into fame's spotlight by the modern phenomenon of reality TV.

Jade stood apart from the reality show pack because she was humble enough to know how lucky she was – and savvy enough to make a fortune from it.

A picture of Jade on The Sun's front page would add tens of thousands to the sale. But that's not why we'll miss her.

The truth is, we liked Jade. She was tenacious, optimistic, a fantastic mum to two smashing boys and hugely courageous despite the many obstacles life threw in her path, including the one she was ultimately unable to conquer.

She had a good heart too. Even Shilpa Shetty knew that, despite their run-in during Celebrity Big Brother. It was a measure of Jade's magnetism that that infamous episode did nothing to damage her long-term popularity.

Above all else, Jade was simply great fun.

The Sun is proud to have worked with MatrixPhotos.com to put together this book in her memory and to be raising funds for her chosen cancer charity. We hope you enjoy it.

John Edwards, Picture Editor
The Sun

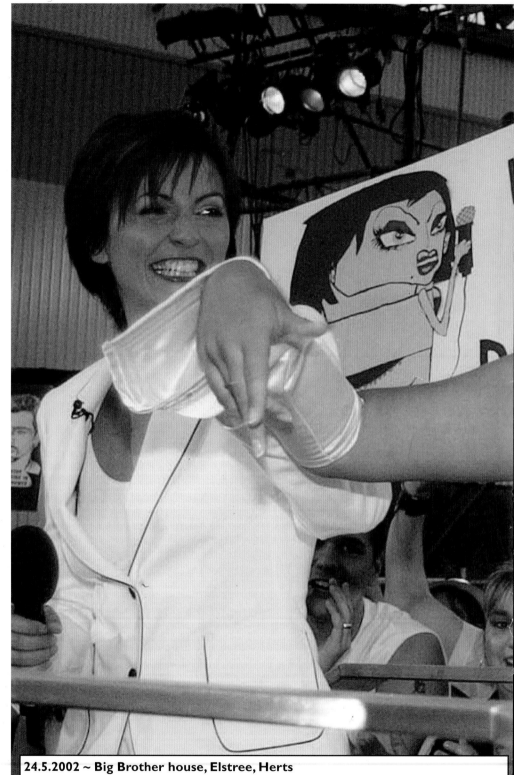

24.5.2002 ~ Big Brother house, Elstree, Herts
The journey begins . . . Jade enters the house (top left), is greeted by Davina McCall and her new legion of fans after finishing fourth (main picture) on July 26 and is treated to a ride through her native Bermondsey, South London, aboard the Sun bus on August 1.

19.12.2002 ~ Gravesend, Kent
Her first major job after leaving Big Brother, in panto as the Wicked Queen in Snow White.

MAIN PICTURE:
23.6.2003 ~ Harlow, Essex
Jade and partner Jeff Brazier step out for the first
time with new baby Bobby, their first child.

MAIN PICTURE, OPPOSITE PAGE
3.8.2003 ~ Hyde Park, London
Out with Bobby again, this time with Jeff, a keen
footballer, nursing a leg injury.

FAR RIGHT, OPPOSITE PAGE
29.8.2003 ~ Sawbridgeworth, Herts
Another romantic day out.

31.10.2003 ~ Harlow, Essex
Jade and Jeff run out of ice while holding a Hallowe'en party and have to dash to Tesco's in full costume, with Bobby dressed as a pumpkin, to get some more.

20.1.2004 ~ New York City
Her first taste of the high life, at the top of the Empire State Building in a freezing Manhattan January. Jade told us she wanted to go to the Big Apple and show Bobby the sights, and we were happy to take her. The trip took in traditional New York activities: sightseeing, shopping in the snow, eating hot-dogs and catching a yellow cab.

6.3.2004 ~ Harlow, Essex
Jade was always determined her boys would have a better education than she did, and she started early with Bobby, showing him the kids' book "Whose Nose?" while on an afternoon out at the park. Once the hard work was over the little lad was treated to a ride down the slide with his mum.

33

7.3.2004 ~ Canvey Island, Essex
Bobby's first time watching dad Jeff play football, for Canvey Island.

28.4.2004 ~ Colchester Zoo, Essex
Her boys' obsession with zoos, farms and animals
in general began on this wonderful day out.

43

17.5.2004 ~ Parliament Green, Westminster
Bobby's first Porsche! Jade bought him the motorised miniature from the Porsche dealership on Park Lane. The lad was overjoyed with it as he drove around the park.

5.6.2004 ~ Southend-on-Sea, Essex
On her birthday, Jade treated all her girlfriends to a day out at Adventure Island. Each was kitted out with a pink hat and a Goody's Girls souvenir top. The picture on pages 50-51 shows three friends, Kelly, Charlene and Jennifer, who would become her bridesmaids five years later.

12.7.2004 ~ Harlow, Essex
Pregnant Jade has a summer clearout ready for the arrival of her second child. Helped by mum Jackiey, she unearths a giant ET, a pair of shears, some old bathroom tiles and a school shirt, signed by all her old schoolmates, which she decided not to throw out.

3.9.2004 ~ Windsor, Berks
Now heavily pregnant, Jade wanted to spoil Bobby with some quality time together before Freddie's arrival and picked the Legoland theme park. Mum Jackiey went along for the fun.

25.10.2004 ~ Strood, Kent
Every young boy loves diggers and Bobby had a whale of a time at the Diggerland theme park. **Overleaf:** The Diggerland trip also saw the first public appearance of Jade's second son Freddie.

8.11.2004 ~ Hertingfordbury, Herts
Jade's quest to give her boys the best possible education began on a crisp autumn morning as she looked around a private school in Herts. In the end she picked another school for Bobby.

27.11.2004 ~ Harlow, Essex
Now a single mum, Jade planned Christmas for herself and the boys, buying a tree at a garden centre and wheeling Bobby around on her trolley.

1.3.2005 ~ Naples, Florida
Never one to forget her roots, Jade treated her old schoolfriends to a fantastic break in the sunshine state.

22.6.2005 ~ Dubai, United Arab Emirates
Trying her hand at surfing at the Wild Wadi Water Park.

27.7.2005 ~ Hertford, Herts
The start of Jade's TV career. Team Jade line up before building Jade's salon, called Ugly's, converted from an old bank. This was for the Living TV series Jade's Salon. **Overleaf:** Bobby and Freddie lend a hand and Jade poses with business partner Carly Walpole.

9.10.2005 ~ Bishops Stortford, Herts
Jade and her friends formed a netball team called Team Brentwood and joined a Sunday league. The venture was short-lived because Jade kept running into trouble with the ref – and because she refused to remove her jewellery!

13.11.2005 ~ Hurghada, Egypt
Freddie took his first steps on this family
holiday to the baking-hot Red Sea resort.
Everyone needed to cool down in the
blistering heat and this water fight with
Bobby did the trick.

9.1.2006 ~ Epping Forest, Essex
Starting what was meant to be a three-month training programme before running the London Marathon. The training lasted somewhat less than three months . . . it was more like three hours!

8.3.2006 ~ Chamonix, France
Jade was determined to go on a "posh" trip like some of the other mums at Bobby's school. So she gave skiing a go in the Alps . . . with mixed results!

16.3.2006 ~ Nassau, Bahamas
Jade's first holiday with new love, and future husband, Jack Tweed. The James Bond movie Casino Royale was being filmed there at the time and Jade insisted on seeing the set.

23.4.2006 ~ Blackheath, South-East London
Lining up with other celebrities at the start of the London Marathon. Everyone knew what would happen next! **Overleaf:** Shattered Jade dropped out after 23 miles and was rescued by the Salvation Army, who took her to a nearby hotel to recover.

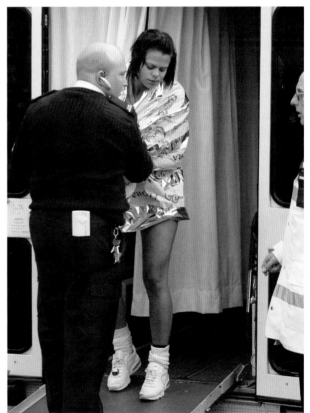

20.5.2006 ~ Cannes, South of France
Jade and pal Carly celeb-spotting during the Cannes film festival. Jade was on her way to Grasse, the French "perfume capital", to pick up her own branded fragrance.

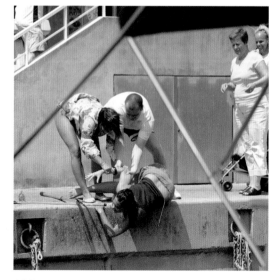

21.5.2006 ~ Cannes harbour, South of France

Her good friend and business partner Carly gave Jade her first look at the star's "Shhh" perfume and managed to drop the bottle in the water. French locals helped a laughing Jade haul Carly to safety after she looked about to fall in while fetching the bottle. The Sun's picture desk was rendered helpless with laughter when the pictures arrived in the office.

11.6.2006 ~ Tantra Nightclub, Central London
Jade dressed to kill at her "tarts and vicars" birthday party.

102

19.6.2006 ~ Embassy Nightclub, Mayfair, London
The launch of Shhh, at Jade's favourite venue Embassy, owned by her good friend Mark Fuller.

6.7.2006 ~ Havana, Cuba
A typical Jade moment. A relaxing afternoon in the sunshine turned into a
fun-filled drama as she playfully turfed Jack out of the hammock.

12.7.2006 ~ Theydon Bois, Essex
Jade, being taught golf by Jack's dad Andy, leapt for joy as she holed a long-range putt.

15.9.2006 ~ Chipping Ongar, Essex
Jade's ex, Jeff, and her boyfriend Jack were together to help Freddie celebrate his second birthday at the leisure centre.

19.9.2006 ~ Venue Theatre, Leicester Square, London
She always wanted to appear on the West End stage, and Jade's dream came true when the producers of the Vegemite Tales invited her to perform a one-off cameo.

1.12.2006 ~ Soho, London
On a romantic weekend off from looking after the boys, Jack treated Jade to some sexy undies on a shopping trip in the capital.

3.1.2007 ~ Isle of Dogs, East London
Leaving by helicopter for the Celebrity Big Brother house in Elstree.

23.1.2007 ~ Chipping Ongar, Essex
Jade's joy was clear to see as she was reunited with her boys for the first time after her life-changing appearance on Celebrity Big Brother.

6.2.2007 ~ Watton, Norfolk
Escaping the limelight for a weekend of reflection amid the turmoil of the Shilpa Shetty row. Jade took the family to Jack's uncle's estate, where they spent the afternoons walking, painting and quad-biking. As usual Jade made sure she had the appropriate accessories . . . country boots and Barbour jacket.

26.2.2007 ~ Delhi, India
On a visit to India to make a donation to the Railway Children charity, Jade wanted to take in some of the city's iconic sights and experiences.

27.2.2007 ~ Delhi, India
Jade meant her visit to India to be private and low-key. But in the wake of the Celebrity Big Brother row it took no time at all before she was being mobbed by the Indian media.

11.4.2007 ~ Enfield, North London
Jade always kept her feet on the ground, no matter how famous she became. She and Jack did the weekly shop together, like any other couple . . . in this case at the Makro cash-and-carry.

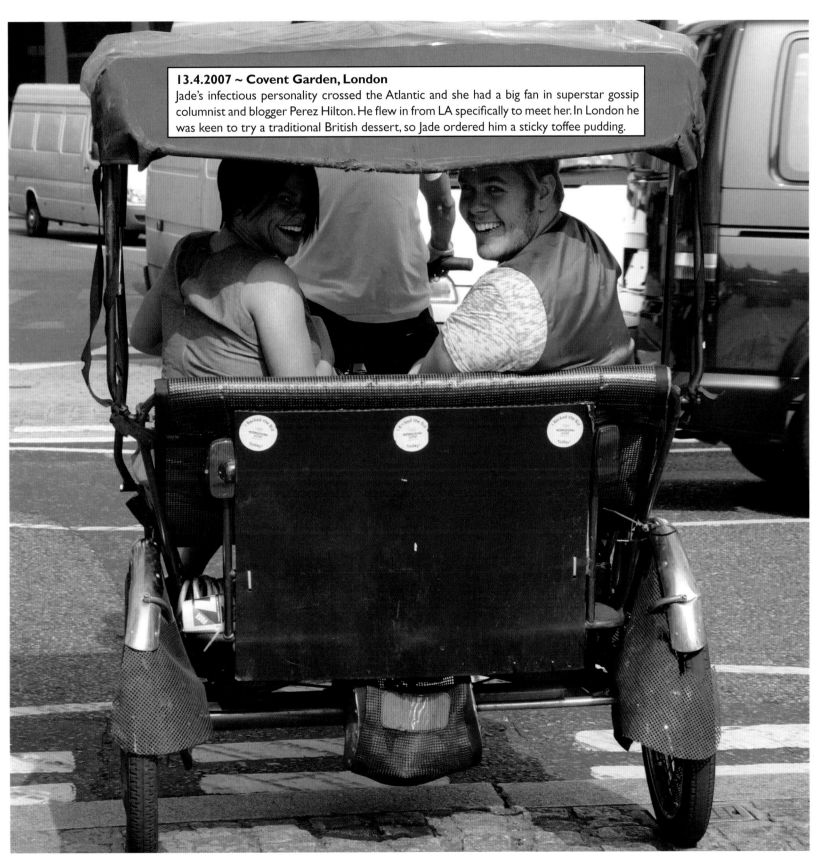

13.4.2007 ~ Covent Garden, London

Jade's infectious personality crossed the Atlantic and she had a big fan in superstar gossip columnist and blogger Perez Hilton. He flew in from LA specifically to meet her. In London he was keen to try a traditional British dessert, so Jade ordered him a sticky toffee pudding.

15.4.2007 ~ Tobago, West Indies
Soaking up the Caribbean sunshine and paddling a dinghy on a holiday with Jack and the boys.

16.4.2007 ~ Tobago, West Indies
The holiday villa Jade rented fell victim to a spate of bush fires sweeping the island. Jade was forced to tackle the blaze in her hedge with the help of some locals.

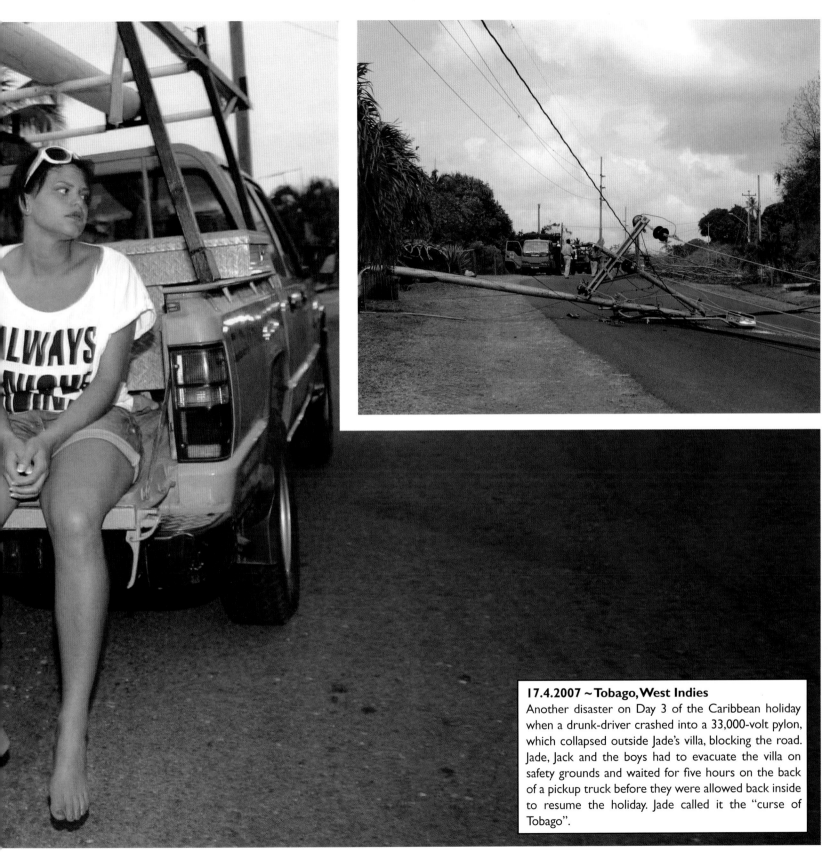

17.4.2007 ~ Tobago, West Indies
Another disaster on Day 3 of the Caribbean holiday when a drunk-driver crashed into a 33,000-volt pylon, which collapsed outside Jade's villa, blocking the road. Jade, Jack and the boys had to evacuate the villa on safety grounds and waited for five hours on the back of a pickup truck before they were allowed back inside to resume the holiday. Jade called it the "curse of Tobago".

19.6.2007 ~ King's Lynn, Norfolk

Part of Jade's infectious charm was that she was so accident-prone. She had already passed her driving test once, but had to retake it because she forgot to send off the appropriate documents before the DVLA deadline. Jade picked Norfolk for the retake because, she said, the landscape was flat, the roads were wide and it was deserted. Needless to say, she passed second time as well as first!

153

18.7.2007 ~ Hertford, Herts
Jade goes blonde.

26.8.2007 ~ Marbella, Spain
Marbella with its various beach clubs was the favourite holiday destination for Jade and her friends.

2.9.2007 ~ Warwick, Warwickshire
Jade wanted a traditional English holiday, so we suggested narrow-boating along the canals of the Midlands. We rented her a boat for four days and ended up giving it back after two. Jade didn't take to canal life ... too many locks, she said. She didn't fancy sleeping on the boat, either. She preferred hotels.

3.1.2008 ~ Abu Dhabi, United Arab Emirates
Jade flew out to visit her friend Mark Fuller, who was opening a new branch of his London nightclub, Embassy. Jade couldn't stop laughing at the hotel suite he put her in ... it was bigger than her house.

6.2.2008 ~ Connaught Water, Epping Forest, Essex
As she joined the ranks of showbiz millionaires, Jade felt she deserved one major treat, and got herself the standard motoring accessory for wealthy Essex girls . . . a £140,000 soft-top Bentley.

11.3.2008 ~ Epping Forest, Essex
Close friend and personal trainer Kevin Adams put Jade through her paces as she launched a new fitness drive.

8.4.2008 ~ Bognor Regis, West Sussex
Another of Jade's traditional British holidays, taking the boys to Butlins over the Easter break.

18.5.2008 ~ Millwall Football Club, South-East London
Playing in a charity football match at The Den alongside pop star Pete Doherty.

29.7.2008 ~ Mayfair, London
The Jade brand continues, with the launch of her second perfume named "Controversial". It was déjà vu . . . just like with her first scent, Shhh, Jade managed to drop the bottle on the ground. The perfume went on to be a huge success, just as Shhh was.

27.8.2008 ~ Pontfaen, Pembrokeshire, West Wales
The best holiday of Jade's life, as she later admitted . . . and the most poignant too. She had been diagnosed with cancer and knew she faced chemotherapy and a gruelling battle for her life. This, she knew, would be her last family holiday for a long while, and possibly for ever. And she made the most of it in idyllic, rural West Wales.

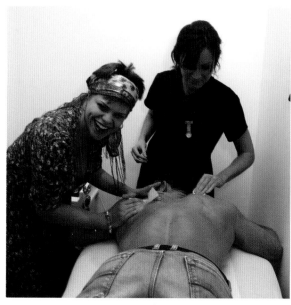
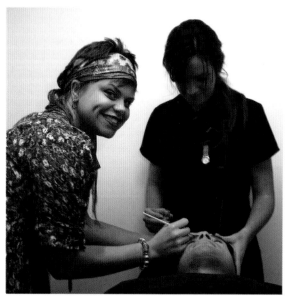
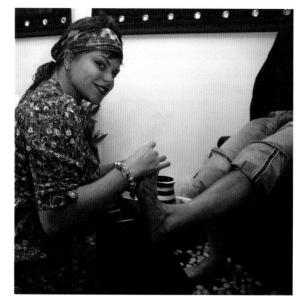

15.10.2008 ~ Epping, Essex
The Goody empire continued to expand, despite the star undergoing chemotherapy. She went into partnership with Julie Morris in a new men's grooming salon. Despite her ill health, Jade's optimism still shone through in these pictures.

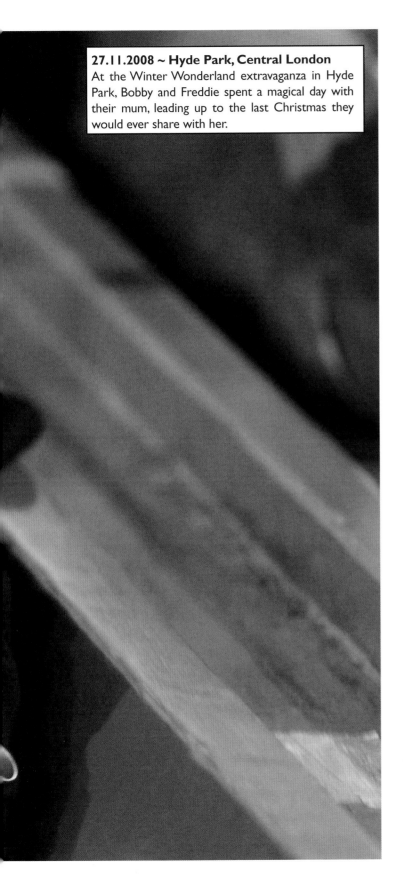

27.11.2008 ~ Hyde Park, Central London
At the Winter Wonderland extravaganza in Hyde Park, Bobby and Freddie spent a magical day with their mum, leading up to the last Christmas they would ever share with her.

7.12.2008 ~ Lakeside, Essex
Despite her cancer treatment Jade still somehow found the energy for both work and family life. A huge crowd turned out to see her launch her second autobiography "Catch A Falling Star" and queued for signed copies. **Overleaf:** Jade asked us to shoot a picture for the back of her book. This was the result.

17.12.2008 ~ Lincoln, Lincs
With her boys at the opening night of her second panto stint, again as the Wicked Queen in Snow White, this time alongside Coronation Street's Curly Watts (actor Kevin Kennedy). Jade's ill health got the better of her not long after these pictures were taken and she had to pull out after only a few performances.

13.1.2009 ~ Tenerife, Canary Islands
Jade's friend and business associate Bob Coleman invited the star to spend a few relaxing days at his villa. She swam in the ocean, played football on the beach, visited the zoo with the kids and went on a catamaran trip in the sunset. Her expression occasionally betrayed the pain she was suffering, but more often than not she smiled bravely.

20.1.2009 ~ Upshire, Essex
Her hair lost through chemotherapy, Jade showed off her baldness for the first time at her home alongside her friend Kevin Adams.

27.1.2009 ~ Wayland Prison, Norfolk
The kiss that said it all, as Jade's true love jack was released from a four-mounth prison term. The couple were reunited ready for the hardest days of her life.

15.2.2009 ~ Chelsea Embankment, South-West London
On a peaceful Sunday morning beside the Thames, Jack declared his love for Jade, now wheelchair-bound, and asked her to be his wife. Her smile said it all.

227

20.2.2009 ~ Upshire, Essex
Here come the girls! Jade's bridesmaids (left to right, Caroline, Charlene, Jennifer and Kelly), with bald wigs in support of their great friend, get ready for the big day.

20.2.2009 ~ Mayfair, Central London
A girl's gotta smile! Jade and her bridesmaids have their teeth whitened ready for the wedding.

20.2.2009 ~ Upshire, Essex
One of the most beautiful and heartfelt pictures of Jade we ever took, kissing Jack after arriving home from London.

1.3.2009 ~ Chelsea, South-West London
Jade, being treated at the Royal Marsden Hospital, was helping choose pictures for this book when she suddenly said: "Let's do some more right here," and gave us a jokey pose alongside her good friend Kate Jackson. "We can end the book with these," Jade said.

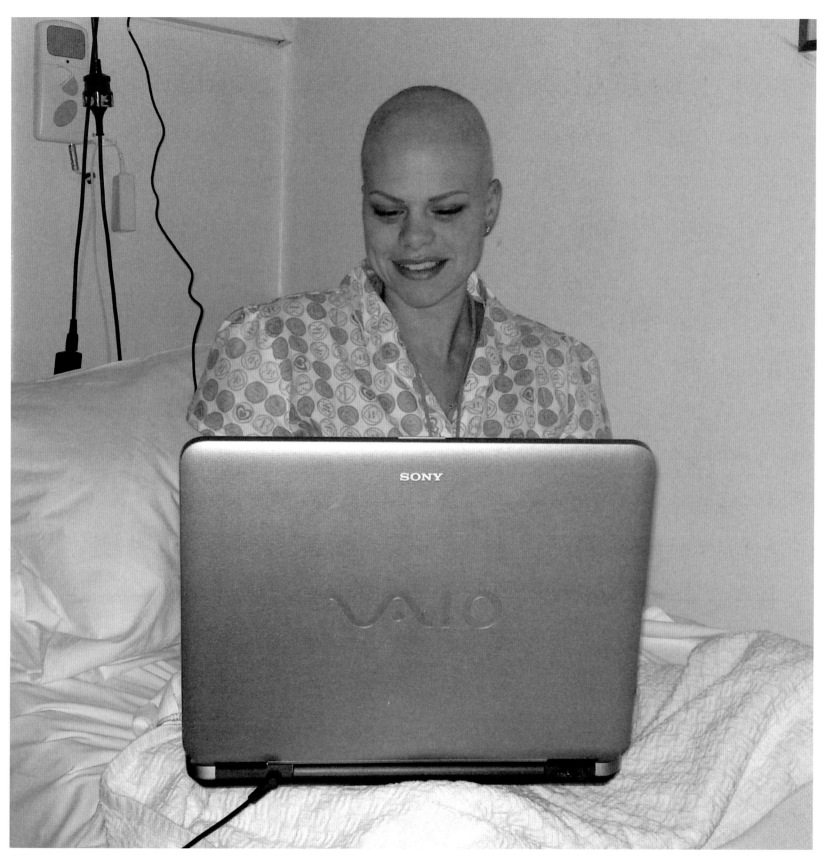

THANKS TO:

Jade Goody and all her family and friends
pictured in the book.

Paul Hennessy, Wayne Buckland,
Steve Spiller, Grant Buchanan,
Glenn Gratton, Trevor Adams,
Ray Collins, Dean Cranston and
Enfoque, who kindly gave consent for
their pictures to be used.

Justine and the team at HandE Publishers.

John Perry and John Edwards
from The Sun.

Trevor Adams, John Churchill,
Jon Bushell and the team at MatrixPhotos.com
for their hard work in the preparation of
this book.